The Peculiar Stories Behind Raining Cats and Dogs

and Other Idioms

Published by The Child's World®
1980 Lookout Drive • Mankato, MN 56003-1705
800-599-READ • www.childsworld.com

Acknowledgments
The Child's World®: Mary Berendes, Publishing Director
The Design Lab: Design and production
Red Line Editorial: Editorial direction

Design elements: Kirsty Pargeter/iStockphoto

ISBN 9781614732358
LCCN 2012932813

Printed in the United States of America
Mankato, MN
July 2012
PA02118

Contents

STICK-IN-THE-MUD

MEANING: A person who is a **stick-in-the-mud** is not interested in excitement and change.

ORIGIN: This phrase dates to the 1700s or earlier. It refers to being stuck in actual mud.

EXAMPLE: Jose wasn't excited about the field trip to the marshmallow factory. His friends called him a **stick-in-the-mud**.

COLD TURKEY

MEANING: If you quit something **cold turkey**, you quit it suddenly and all at once.

ORIGIN: The origin of this phrase is not known for sure. It may be related to the idiom "talk turkey," which means to talk about serious business. Today, the use of "turkey" would mean to get serious about an addiction.

EXAMPLE: Maggie decided to quit **cold turkey**. After this last slice, she would never eat pizza again.

THE BIG CHEESE

MEANING: Someone who is **the big cheese** is the most powerful or important person in a group.

ORIGIN: The likely origin of this phrase has nothing to do with cheese. The Hindi word *chiz*, meaning "thing," was used by British people in India in the phrase "the real chiz." "Chiz" was misheard as "cheese," and Americans later adopted the phrase as "the big cheese."

EXAMPLE: Sarah was **the big cheese** in her model rocket club. Her rockets always soared the highest.

SEA CHANGE

MEANING: A **sea change** is a major change.

ORIGIN: This phrase comes from William Shakespeare's play *The Tempest.* The phrase refers to the change that happens to something put underwater for a long time.

EXAMPLE: Jasmine's stuffed animal went through a **sea change** while it was lost in a snow bank all winter.

BELLS AND WHISTLES

MEANING: Bells and whistles are unnecessary but interesting features added to attract attention.

ORIGIN: Two possible origins seem likely. The first is from trains, which use bells and whistles as signals. The second is from early movie theaters, which used bells and whistles to make sound effects.

EXAMPLE: Kent's new calculator had all the **bells and whistles**. It could add and subtract and even do advanced calculus.

TAKE A PAGE OUT OF SOMEONE'S BOOK

MEANING: To **take a page out of someone's book** is to do or say what they would do.

ORIGIN: This phrase uses a book to represent a person's personality. When you take a page out of another person's book, you copy their personality in some way.

EXAMPLE: Abdul **took a page out of Hugo's book**. He wore the same clothes as Hugo, all the way down to the glow-in-the dark suspenders.

AHEAD OF THE CURVE

MEANING: A person who is **ahead of the curve** is able to foresee or anticipate future changes.

ORIGIN: This phrase probably comes from the US military, referring to the power curve of an airplane. The power curve is represented by a graph. This graph shows speed and engine power. You are in a better position if your speed and engine power are on the correct side of the graph's curve.

EXAMPLE: Marty was **ahead of the curve** in his history class. He looked forward in the textbook to see what happened next.

GO THE WAY OF THE DODO

MEANING: To **go the way of the dodo** is to disappear or go unused.

ORIGIN: The dodo bird was an animal that went extinct in the 1600s.

EXAMPLE: Stu's clothing style **went the way of the dodo**. It hasn't been popular since last month.

CUTE AS A BUG'S EAR

MEANING: A person or thing that is as **cute as a bug's ear** is extremely cute.

ORIGIN: This phrase is one of many that describe small things as cute. Others include "cute as a button" and "cute as a kitten."

EXAMPLE: Miko's mother always said Miko was as **cute as a bug's ear** in public. This embarrassed Miko greatly.

THE LION'S SHARE

MEANING: The lion's share of something is the largest portion.

ORIGIN: The phrase comes from Aesop's fables, ancient stories that teach moral lessons. These stories have animals for characters, and the lion is one of the most powerful of them.

EXAMPLE: Keisha was hungry, so she ate **the lion's share** of the popcorn at the movies.

ACHILLES' HEEL

MEANING: A person's **Achilles' heel** is his or her weak spot.

ORIGIN: This phrase comes from the mythical story of the Greek hero Achilles. It was said that his mother dipped him into magical waters as a baby, making him invincible. However, she held him by his heel, so that became his only weak spot.

EXAMPLE: Louis was great at multiplication, but his **Achilles' heel** was long division.

IN THE DOLDRUMS

MEANING: A person who is **in the doldrums** is feeling sad, slow, or tired.

ORIGIN: In the 1800s, a "doldrum" was the opposite of a "tantrum," with "dol" coming from the word "dull." Later it was used to describe an area of the ocean where winds are weak, making sailing difficult.

EXAMPLE: Lyle was **in the doldrums**. The next book by his favorite author wouldn't come out until next year.

INSIDE BASEBALL

MEANING: Discussions that are **inside baseball** include details interesting only to experts.

ORIGIN: This idiom comes from a less-exciting style of playing baseball. This style may seem boring to people who don't know much about baseball, but it is interesting to experts.

EXAMPLE: Taylor liked to talk about even the smallest details of the moon landings, but to some of her friends it was all **inside baseball**.

TAKE IT WITH A GRAIN OF SALT

MEANING: When you **take something with a grain of salt**, you have some doubts about what you are told.

ORIGIN: This idiom comes from putting salt on your food to make it taste better. It refers to covering up some doubts about what you are told to make it easier to accept.

EXAMPLE: Mona **took it with a grain of salt** when Cecil told her his brother was a famous actor.

BURY THE HATCHET

MEANING: To **bury the hatchet** is to settle your differences with an enemy.

ORIGIN: This idiom comes from a ritual performed by some Native American tribes. Tribal chiefs would bury hatchets when they made a peace agreement.

EXAMPLE: The rival schools' basketball teams decided to finally **bury the hatchet**. They all went out for frosty chocolate milkshakes.

SALAD DAYS

MEANING: Someone's **salad days** are their youthful days when they are inexperienced but hopeful and eager.

ORIGIN: This phrase was invented by William Shakespeare in his play *Antony and Cleopatra*. It is a reference to the green color of salad, using one meaning of "green" that suggests youth.

EXAMPLE: Rex's grandfather told him to enjoy his **salad days**.

LET THE CAT OUT OF THE BAG

MEANING: To **let the cat out of the bag** is to tell a secret.

ORIGIN: This phrase likely refers to a cat's desire to get out of an actual bag. This is similar to a person's desire to tell a secret.

EXAMPLE: Lionel finally **let the cat out of the bag**. He told his sister Stacy what their parents bought her for her birthday.

KEEP YOUR EYES PEELED

MEANING: To **keep your eyes peeled** is to be alert and attentive.

ORIGIN: This phrase first appeared in the United States around 1850. It refers to taking off any real or imaginary covering of the eyes that might make it more difficult to see.

EXAMPLE: Scott had to **keep his eyes peeled**. The comet could appear at any second.

FACE THE MUSIC

MEANING: To **face the music** is to accept the bad consequences of your actions.

ORIGIN: The origin of this phrase is uncertain. It may come from the military, where drummers used to stand at the front of a group of soldiers. Another theory is that it came from theaters, where actors had to face the orchestra between them and the audience.

EXAMPLE: It was time for Luann to **face the music**. She had to tell her parents that she broke the new chandelier.

COME OUT OF THE WOODWORK

MEANING: When something **comes out of the woodwork**, it appears or emerges. This phrase usually refers to something unpleasant.

ORIGIN: The phrase refers to insects and spiders coming out of the woodwork of a house.

EXAMPLE: Problems with Nick's new computer kept **coming out of the woodwork**. First the sound stopped working, and then smoke began coming out of the back.

TIE THE KNOT

MEANING: To **tie the knot** is to get married.

ORIGIN: Knots have been used in many cultures to represent a connection between people. Also, actual knots are a part of some kinds of wedding ceremonies.

EXAMPLE: Helen's older brother and his fiancé were planning to **tie the knot** on March 14th. Helen was more excited to eat cake at the wedding than she was for the ceremony, though.

CHEW THE FAT

MEANING: To **chew the fat** is to talk casually about something unimportant.

ORIGIN: When you chew actual fat from a piece of meat, the movement of the jaw is similar to when you are talking casually.

EXAMPLE: Santiago liked to **chew the fat** with his friends, talking for hours about sports and video games.

PICK SOMEONE'S BRAIN

MEANING: To **pick someone's brain** is to speak with a person in order to learn about something he or she knows.

ORIGIN: This phrase uses the word "pick" in the same sense as "picking fruit." It refers to gathering someone's knowledge.

EXAMPLE: "Can I **pick your brain** about this science homework?" Todd asked Maria. He knew Maria was an expert on dinosaurs.

HOUSE WARMING

MEANING: A **house warming** is a celebration held for the new owners of a house.

ORIGIN: Originally, this phrase meant to literally warm up a new home. Eventually, it gained its current meaning.

EXAMPLE: Hank went to a **house warming** party for his friend Gil, whose parents had recently bought a new house.

RAINING CATS AND DOGS

MEANING: If it is **raining cats and dogs**, it is raining very heavily.

ORIGIN: There are many theories about the origin of this common idiom. It may come from European myths in which cats represented rain and dogs represented wind. It may also refer to the dirty city of 1700s London, when a heavy rain would wash trash and animals down the streets.

EXAMPLE: It was really **raining cats and dogs** out there! If it rained any more, Samantha would have to canoe home from school.

STRAIGHT FROM THE HORSE'S MOUTH

MEANING: Information that is **straight from the horse's mouth** is from the most reliable source.

ORIGIN: This phrase came from horse racing. An old joke said that the best information about who would win the race would come from asking the horses themselves.

EXAMPLE: The news came **straight from the horse's mouth**. Evan's grandmother told him she would be coming to visit the next week.

GREEN WITH ENVY

MEANING: Someone who is **green with envy** is very envious.

ORIGIN: It was once thought that a person's face turned green when they were jealous. It comes from the phrase "green-eyed jealousy" used in William Shakespeare's play *The Merchant of Venice*.

EXAMPLE: Julius was **green with envy**. His friend Mindy had a new cell phone. Now he wanted one, too.

HEAD OVER HEELS

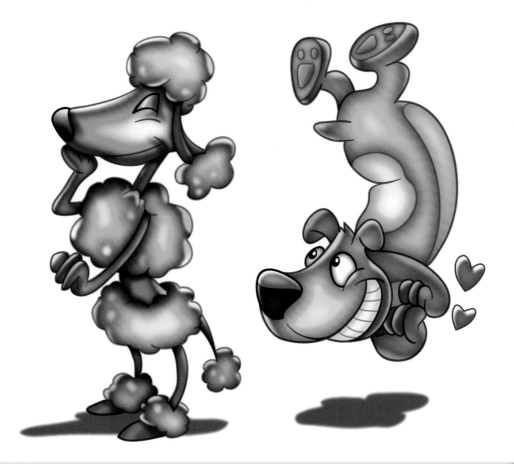

MEANING: A person who is **head over heels** has fallen in love suddenly and dramatically.

ORIGIN: This phrase originally started as "heels over head," suggesting the person is so struck by love that he or she falls over. It was mixed up into "head over heels" in the 1700s.

EXAMPLE: Martin was **head over heels** for his new pet platypus.

About the Author

Arnold Ringstad lives in Minneapolis, where he graduated from the University of Minnesota in 2011. He enjoys reading books about space exploration and playing board games with his girlfriend. Writing about idioms makes him as happy as a clam.

About the Illustrator

Dan McGeehan loves being an illustrator. His art appears in many magazines and children's books. He currently lives in Oklahoma.